The Birth of Christ

Luke: *Chapter 2:6—2:20*
Matthew: *Chapter 1:18—2:15*

When Joseph and Mary reached Bethlehem in Judea, they found that the city was already full of people who, like them, had come to have their names enrolled due to the order of the Roman Emperor, Augustus Caesar. Joseph was worried thinking about where they would stay that night as Mary was in her advanced stage of pregnancy.

As all the inns were full, Joseph and his wife took shelter in a stable, where the cattle were kept. It was here that the Son of God, Jesus was born. The little baby was laid in a manger in which the cattle were fed.

On that night some shepherds were tending their sheep in a field near Bethlehem. Suddenly a great light shone upon them, and they saw an angel standing before them. They were filled with fear.

3

But the angel said to the shepherds, 'Do not be afraid for I bring you news of great joy! In Bethlehem, the *Saviour* is born. He is a new-born baby, lying in a manger at an inn.' And then, they saw that the sky above them was filled with angels, all singing praises of God.

The next moment the angels were gone! The shepherds said to one another, 'Let us go at once to Bethlehem and see the divine child.'
On reaching Bethlehem, they told Mary and Joseph how they had seen the angels, and what praises they had heard about this baby.

When the divine child was eight days old, Joseph and Mary named him *Jesus,* as the angel had told them. Joseph and Mary stayed in Bethlehem with baby Jesus for sometime. With time they shifted from the stable to a proper room.

Meanwhile, in a country east of Judea, many miles away lived some very wise men who studied the stars. One night they saw a strange star shining in the sky. They at once knew that the coming of this star meant that a king was soon to be born in the land of Judea. These men felt a call of God to go to Judea to see this new-born king.

And so the three wise men made a long journey, with camels and horses to the land of Judea. They reached just at the time when Jesus was born in Bethlehem. As soon as they were in Judea they thought that every one would know about the divine baby. But to their surprise, no one could tell them about him.

The news of the coming of these wise men was sent to Herod, the king, who was then a very old man. He ruled the land of Judea, under the Emperor at Rome, Augustus Caesar. Herod was a wicked man. When he heard about the birth of Jesus who was meant to be king, he feared that he would lose his own kingdom. So, he made up his mind to kill this new king.

Like all others Herod tried to find out who Jesus was. He asked, 'Can you tell me where Christ, the King of Israel is to be born?' He was told that Jesus was to be born in Bethlehem of Judea as forecasted by the prophets.

Herod wasted no more time. He sent for the wise men from the east and met them alone. He found from them the time at which they had first seen the star. Then he said to them, 'Go to Bethlehem, and look for the little child. And when you find him, let me know so that I also may come and worship him.'

So the wise men started towards Bethlehem. Suddenly they saw the star shining again upon the road before them. The three wise men were glad and followed the star until it led them to the very house where the little child was.

When they saw the divine child they knew at once that this was the King, and they worshipped him as the Lord. They gave their offerings of gold, frankincense and myrrh which they had brought for the royal child. These three wise men were the Magi.

That night God came in the dream of the three wise men, telling them not to go back to Herod, but to go home by another way. They obeyed the Lord. So King Herod did not know who the divine child was.

Meanwhile Joseph too had a dream in which God told him to take his son and his wife to Egypt as King Herod would try to kill the child. Joseph obeyed at once and they lived safely in Egypt.